how to use
audio-visual materials

how to use
AUDIO-VISUAL
MATERIALS

JOHN W. BACHMAN

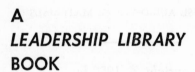

A
LEADERSHIP LIBRARY
BOOK

Association Press, New York

table of contents

HOW TO USE AUDIO-VISUAL MATERIALS

Copyright © 1956 by
National Board of Young Men's Christian Associations

Association Press, 291 Broadway, New York 7, N. Y.

$1.00

Library of Congress catalog card number: 56-6453

Printed in the United States of America

1

when are audio-visual materials useful?

Are audio-visual materials worth the bother they cause you? You are expected, by public-opinion pressures, to say yes. Our society is exposed so continually to the mass media that the power of sight and sound seems almost beyond question. Some enthusiasts seem to look upon film projectors as intellectual sun lamps and upon television sets as emotional X-ray machines; they imply that you may convey learning or reduce tensions in proportion to the wattage of your projector bulb or to the frequency response of your loudspeaker.

But you suspect that such extremists may have been blinded by their television picture tubes or deafened by their hi-fi sets or, perhaps, simply intoxicated by the glamour of gadgets. You have seen these materials used when they were nothing but a waste of time. And the foul-ups that can occur! There was the time you blew a fuse and couldn't find a spare . . . and the times the needle stuck on a record . . . and the motion pictures you rent always seem to have bad splices which break in the middle of a showing. It doesn't take many such incidents to drive a leader back to lecturing, or at least to re-examining the question: are audio-visual materials worth the effort, complications, and expense involved in their use?

On the basis of research, experience, and observation, the answer seems to be: yes, it is possible to learn more faster, and remember it longer, *provided* appropriate materials are skillfully used. Your group will not learn more from just any film which happens to be available without cost on a particular night; there must be careful selection from a wide range of materials including the following:

AUDIO	VISUAL		AUDIO-VISUAL
	Non-projected		*Non-projected*
recordings	chalkboards	bulletin boards	puppets
discs	flat pictures	feltboards	drama
tapes	diagrams	objects	field trips
radio	graphs	models	
	maps	mockups	*Projected*
	posters	dioramas	sound filmstrips
	cartoons	turnover charts	sound motion
			pictures
	Projected		television
	slides	opaque materials	
	filmstrips	motion pictures	

You will want to know the distinctive characteristics of each type, and these will be presented in Chapter 2. It is not enough, however, for a good material just to be squirted on the screen or hung from a feltboard; there must be intelligent preparation and follow-up. This, too, will be discussed in later pages.

A prior question, however, concerns your purpose and the relation of audio-visual materials to that purpose. Before you open a catalogue or preview a filmstrip, you should know what you expect a material to contribute to the learning situation in your group. The situation, of course, will be influenced by the nature of the group itself, whether it is a nursery school, a Y club, Scout troop, 4-H club, youth center, campus study group, church school class, service club, child study group, center for the aged or any other group of people who gather in an effort to learn together.

You may have responsibilities for leadership in recreation, in arts and crafts, in service projects, or in discussion and study. In all these areas the members of your group will want to develop individually, and to acquire insights for continued character development and spiritual growth. At various times your more immediate objectives may be to arouse interest, to stimulate discussion, to convey information, to deepen understanding, to influence attitudes, to motivate or to inspire. Since this is not a textbook on the philosophy of education we cannot discuss your objectives at greater length. We must, however, assume that you have defined the goals of your group and your own leadership function. Then you are ready to consider the possible usefulness of audio-visual materials in pursuing these goals.

You will, of course, be using some form of audio-visual material, within a broad definition of the term. Your voice, your appearance, spoken and printed words, all are communicated through eyes and-or ears. In these pages, however, we are focusing attention on the narrower category suggested by the list on page 2. What is distinctive about such materials which may assist you in communicating more effectively than by means of words alone?

they provide experiences

Essentially, audio-visual materials can be helpful because of one basic characteristic: they can provide sensory experiences. Whether they are offering a new experience or recapturing a forgotten one, they may convey, through eyes and ears, a more realistic and vivid impression than words alone are likely to create or recollect.

You may, for example, extend a person's environment by acquainting him with *places and customs* miles or centuries away. Much of the current front-page news is date-lined from parts of the world few of us have visited; both Jewish and Christian heritages have geographical, historical, and cultural foundations foreign to most of us. Good pictures and films can bridge the gaps of space and time with a realism beyond the descriptive power of words.

Learning to know people usually requires more than reading about them. Neither physical descriptions nor biographical data are adequate to communicate personality. Through radio and television, tape and film, your group may become acquainted with persons otherwise scarcely known to them. Parents and teachers can use the same means to observe children at various ages. A series of films portraying the activities of adolescents will help older leaders to remember that behavior which appears to be very unusual may instead be typical.

3

As the armed forces have learned from careful research, *skills* may be taught more effectively by showing how, rather than by telling how to perform them. Whether you are training young people to drive a car, or older men to be church ushers, or children to make lantern slides, there are films, filmstrips, models, or mockups for your purpose.

More complex experiences are the *actions* which bring us into relationship with other people. Here, too, there are "packaged" materials in the form of films or recordings which portray many different situations. Citizens facing problems in their own locality may thus study the efforts of groups elsewhere to meet similar issues. Or, instead, you may wish to undertake field trips and personal interviews, which are closer to being first-hand experiences. You may also consider encouraging your group to engage in forms of creative drama, such as psycho-drama or socio-drama, which enact common personal and social experiences. These may involve participants to the point that they are scarcely removed from original life-experiences.

some are substitutes, which may be advantageous

All the experiences above are, in some sense, substitutes. They are not original and unedited but somewhat contrived and selective. These characteristics give them certain advantages over most first-hand experiences:

1. They are more likely to be available at the time desired.
2. They are likely to be more comprehensive. By careful selection a documentary film or recording may pack into thirty minutes the high points of hours and days of direct observation.
3. They may make possible a sense of perspective seldom achieved in direct participation. A person who is hesitant to discuss his own situation, after seeing a relevant film may be willing to discuss what appear to be the problems of another and gradually come to realize that they are his own also.

some are first-hand experiences

It is not enough, however, to say that audio-visual materials provide vicarious experiences. Many of them, because of their form, provide new, first-hand experiences. Charts and diagrams may visualize relationships in original and distinctive ways. A dramatic production or animated film need not merely *represent* an historical event; it may artistically *create* an event or suggest new interpretations of historical events.

all are likely to be attractive

The very fact that audio-visual materials are experiences in sight and sound makes them attractive. Every teacher who has shown motion pictures in a classroom has observed that passers-by often pause at an open door and occasionally even slip inside. Few lecturers add members to their classes in this way! Human nature makes sensory experiences attractive. Most people prefer, when possible, to see actual mountains, or at least pictures of mountains, rather than the mere word, "mountains."

This attractiveness makes audio-visual materials suspect among some academic purists who seem to maintain that education must be dull to be valid. Admitting that learning is far more than the pursuit of entertainment, most educators and virtually all students believe that there is often a direct relationship between attractiveness and effectiveness of teaching. In the case of audio-visual materials the same characteristic which makes them distinctive and attractive, their ability to provide sensory experiences, also makes them valuable in the learning process.

how they contribute to learning

Experiences provide a *foundation for learning*. To learn, a person must be able to classify his experiences and be able to generalize upon them; he must be able to translate objects and actions into concepts which will allow him to reason, to formulate attitudes and convictions. But first, he must have the experiences. To climb into the atmosphere of abstraction he must have a solid point for his take-off. The child who prayed, "Give us this day our jelly bread and lead us not into Penn

5

Station" was simply unable to leap from nowhere to abstractions such as "daily" and "temptation."

Does this imply that audio-visual materials are useful only for children and illiterates? After we have developed a fairly comprehensive vocabulary, are concrete experiences unnecessary? Not so long as words can be misunderstood or misused. Long-known and frequently used words often need *re-orientation*. Such a common term as "loyalty" may have one connotation for an army officer, another for a teen-age member of a New York street gang, and still another for a poet. "Love" has been portrayed in terms of moonlight, roses, and toothpaste until it is difficult to attach any deeper significance to the word without re-orientation. The same can be said about freedom, justice, power, peace, sin, salvation, and many others you can list. So much has been written about the causes and effects of juvenile delinquency that an unaided group discussion may bog down in jargon. A film, however, depicting the struggle of a child who feels unwanted, will restore focus to the problem. After watching the child's confusion, along with efforts toward rehabilitation, members of a group are less likely to have difficulty in finding meaningful terminology. Common experiences contribute to common understanding.

Similar re-orientation is needed to combat the use of words in stereotyping. Most Americans know there is a "migrant problem" but how much is known beyond this? Films and recordings of the experiences of migrant families reveal their needs as people and not just their classification as census figures. This power, of course, is a two-edged sword; concrete presentations can be used to perpetuate stereotypes as easily as to destroy them, as witnessed by the habitual portrayal in the mass media of certain minority groups in nothing but servile positions. Stereotyping of ideas may be perpetuated in the same way; confining illustration of the term "immorality" to a scene in a bar may reinforce a narrow view of a comprehensive term. To communicate accurately the meaning of an abstraction usually requires more than one concrete reference, and extremely careful selection of those which are used.

Audio-visual materials with their sensory experiences provide, therefore, not only a point of departure but also a point of return for the learning process. Both are needed regularly. Dr. Edgar Dale of Ohio State University explains:

Learning is a process in which the concrete and the abstract interact. We move from the concrete to the abstract and back again to the concrete. It is a shuttling back and forth in which generalizations help us to understand new concrete experiences and the concrete experiences in turn help us to enlarge or refine our generalizations.*

A child accidentally touches a heated iron and learns the meaning of the abstraction "hot." If the original experience is vivid enough he may be able to apply the abstraction to other concrete expressions of "hot," such as a lighted match. Still other experiences will later allow him to refine the meaning of the word.

when to use

Audio-visual materials, then, can provide many different types of new experiences and can recapture old ones. They are useful as experiences for the foundation and re-orientation of learning. Although words are a convenient and economical form of communications shorthand, they may be inaccurate and insufficient; they may suggest sensory impressions, but audio-visual materials correct and intensify these impressions, thus adding a dimension to reality. Audio-visual materials are attractive because they generally appeal more strongly than words alone to the whole person. They should be used under these circumstances:

–when particular experiences are desirable in terms of your purpose. Perhaps members of your group have had no such experiences; perhaps similar experiences they *have* had need reinforcement or cannot be viewed from sufficient perspective.

–when appropriate materials can be located or created to provide these particular experiences. This involves a knowledge of the range of materials and a willingness to search diligently.

---

* *Audio-Visual Methods in Teaching.* Copyright 1954 by The Dryden Press, Inc. Used by permission.

Don't use an audio-visual material for these purposes:

–just to be up to date in your methods. If your group is ready and eager to discuss a current problem, don't frustrate them by showing them a sound filmstrip of another discussion group saying only what your people would willingly say themselves.

–just to entertain, unless your only purpose is to entertain.

–just to keep your group busy. Try to keep the value of the learning experience in proportion to the time involved in the process.

–just because its title sounds relevant to your theme. Preview it in the light of your goals.

–just to give expression to one of your personal hobbies, such as photography or recording. Show your slides to your friends, but don't confuse the slides with program material, unless they really are!

–just because you are unprepared for any other type of presentation. Many horrible experiences have been inflicted on groups under such circumstances.

Deciding when to use and when not to use audio-visual materials is sometimes difficult. The careful selection and intelligent use of appropriate materials add further difficulties, as we shall see. Altogether, audio-visual materials will not ordinarily make leadership easier; but learning will be made easier and leadership more effective, as your group has access to resources otherwise beyond your reach and theirs. Now we are ready to consider what kinds of material may be used in this way.

RESOURCES, CHAPTER ONE

BOOKS

Bryson, Lyman, *The Communication of Ideas* (New York: Harper, 1948).

Dale, Edgar, *Audio-Visual Methods in Teaching* (New York: Dryden Press, rev. ed., 1954).

Grand, Samuel, *Audio-Visual Education in the Jewish Religious School* (Union of American Hebrew Congregations, 1955).

Hockman, William S., *Projected Visual Aids in the Church* (Boston: Pilgrim Press, 1947).

Rogers, William L., and Vieth, Paul H., *Visual Aids in the Church* (Christian Education Press, 1946).

Schramm, Wilbur, *The Process and Effects of Mass Communication* (Urbana, Ill.: University of Illinois Press, 1954).

Tower, Howard E., *Church Use of Audio-Visuals* (Nashville, Tenn.: Abingdon Press, 1951).

Wittich, Walter A., and Schuller, Charles F., *Audio-Visual Materials, Their Nature and Use* (New York: Harper, 1953).

PROJECTED MATERIALS

Audio-Visual Materials in Teaching, sound motion picture, B&W or color, 14 min., Coronet Films.

Let Them See, 74-frame filmstrip, B&W, Visual Education Fellowship.

New Tools for Learning, sound motion picture, B&W, 19 min., Encyc. Brit. Films.

The Use of Visual Method in the Church, 91-frame filmstrip with records, color, Congregational Christian Churches.

PERIODICALS

Audio-Visual Communication Review, quarterly, DAVI, 1201 16th St., N.W., Washington 6, D. C.

Educational Screen—Audio-Visual Guide, monthly, Sept.-June, 64 E. Lake St., Chicago 1, Ill.

Instructional Materials, monthly, Oct.-June, DAVI, 1201 16th St., N.W., Washington 6, D. C.

VEF Newsletter, quarterly, Visual Education Fellowship, National Council of Churches, 257 Fourth Avenue, New York 10, N. Y.

2

what types can be used?

After deciding that a particular audio-visual experience is desirable for your group, you will want to consider which type of material can best provide the experience. Should you use a chalkboard or a filmstrip? A tape recording or a motion picture? A feltboard or a flat picture? You can take advantage of the wealth of audio-visual resources only if you know the possibilities and limitations of each type.

audio materials

The term "audio" is sometimes swallowed in "audio-visual" and almost overlooked, except in a supporting role as sound for motion pictures and television. As someone quipped, "You cannot whistle an algebraic formula." But neither can some whistles be reduced to equations! Both the auditory and visual stimuli have distinctive functions.

Listening experiences provided by radio and recordings offer these *advantages*:

1. The voice is frequently the most revealing expression of human personality.
2. Music is essentially a listening experience.
3. Necessary scenery, properties, costumes, and weather conditions may be suggested by the imagination, stimulated by inexpensive sound effects, narration, and dialogue.
4. The mental pictures thus conceived may vary with the individual. This is especially convenient in dealing with Biblical themes, where many people have strong preconceptions.
5. Unnecessary scenic details may be omitted, allowing the sound to concentrate on fundamental principles.

Disadvantages are these:

1. With nothing to watch, listeners are more subject to distractions, thus limiting their attention-span.

2. Listeners are likely to imagine only those visual elements which they have already seen; it is difficult to suggest new visual experiences through the ears alone.

3. Some concepts may be portrayed more clearly in visual than in auditory terms. Maps, for example, make clear at a glance relationships which would be difficult, if not impossible, to describe orally.

Radio and disc recordings, whether 78, 45, or 33⅓ rpm, differ in these respects:

Radio		Records
Offers resources beyond any record collection	-but-	Can be scheduled whenever desired, not just when broadcast
Is less expensive than record collection	-but-	Can be played many times
Its immediacy is attractive	-but-	Can be studied in advance

The tape recorder combines most of the advantages of both radio and records, along with some of its own:

1. Broadcasts can be recorded and filed to be played when convenient, so long as they are not used for commercial purposes.

2. Since the tape can be played many times, then perhaps erased and re-used, the process is comparatively inexpensive.

3. Tapes can be played in advance, interrupted, and replayed—thus making up for the loss of immediacy suffered by a few programs such as news and special events.

4. Tape makes possible a satisfactory quality of local recording at less cost than was possible with disc recorders.

5. Splicing and editing are simple tasks.

The tape recorder has become recognized as one of the most useful and versatile of instructional materials.*[1] Along with radio and records, it is being used for the following purposes:

1. To bring from a distance, or even from the past, speakers who would be unable to address your local group in person. Some of these resources are available in tape and record libraries, others may be taken off the air, still others may be secured by individual request.

---

* All *numbered* resources appear at the end of the chapter.

2. To enrich the local program with nationally produced dramas and documentaries.

3. To collect broadcast commercials, news, and other programs for propaganda analysis, thus contributing to the development of discriminating listening.

4. To bring national panels, forums, and town meetings into the local group to stimulate discussion.

5. To preserve local discussions for later analysis by leader and participants.

6. To exchange local programs with other groups.

7. To file a spare program or sermon as protection against sudden illness of a leader.

8. To maintain oral contact with group members away or ill.

9. To preserve meetings, conventions, and worship services for shut-ins and other absentees to hear later. (Tapes of business meetings are also useful to a secretary in compiling minutes.)

10. To provide music for worship, for social functions, or for study. The wide choice of commercial discs or tapes, along with developments in "high-fidelity" and binaural (two-ear) recording, stimulate this use.

11. To preserve events such as dedications and anniversaries for archives.

12. To prepare attractive annual reports, using selected segments of tape used during the year.

13. To preserve a wedding ceremony. The playback can be a moving experience for a couple who probably heard little of the original service!

14. To provide an exact record of counseling sessions for private, analytical use by the counselor. As psychiatrists have noted, the pitch, tempo, volume, and inflection of the voice may be as significant as words.

15. To allow speakers and singers to hear themselves as others hear them, making possible critical group or private analysis.

16. To assist in language training, especially for drill in pronunciation, partially substituting for the conversational experience essential to acquiring a speaking knowledge of a language.

17. To record dramatic rehearsals and performances for interpretative analysis.

18. To provide sound effects for drama and interpretative readings.

19. To record sound track for filmstrips, slide-sets and films, thus producing a combination audio-visual material, which will be discussed in the following section.

With some experimentation you will be able to add to the list above.

If you do not have the necessary equipment for such projects, you will wonder how to decide which machine to purchase. In general, select a reputable dealer who will be able to make repairs when they become necessary. Specifically, each type of equipment has certain features which should be evaluated in relation to your intended uses. In a *tape recorder*, for example, you will consider these factors:

–quality of reproduction. How closely do the recordings resemble the original sounds? The quality is likely to be roughly proportional to the cost—and also to the weight!

–recording speeds in inches per second: 1⅞, 3¾, 7½, 15. The slower the speed, the longer a recording can be made on a reel of tape. The faster the speed, the better the quality. For music or even for careful study of the speaking voice, any speed below 7½ generally is unsatisfactory. Two-speed machines give you greater flexibility.

–single or dual track. A dual-track machine (recording on only half the width of the tape in one direction, then reversing and using the other half) saves tape, but makes splicing and editing difficult or impossible.

–speedy forward and rewind action, desirable for all purposes.

–constant speed of motor and dependable brakes. You will have to depend on your dealer at this point, or on the analysis of mechanically competent friends.

–ease of operation, especially important if many different persons are to operate the mechanism.

–an index counter, which is helpful for editing or "spotting" sections.

–a playback system which operates when the reels are moved manually across the head. This is most helpful in editing.

–a monitor system which can be operated during recording. This is necessary only if you plan to undertake complicated productions without the facilities of a control room.

Leading manufacturers of tape recorders and other types of equipment to be mentioned in these pages are listed in the reference section at the end of this chapter.[2]

For best recording results, you should use good-quality tape. In poor tape the iron oxide is not tightly bound to its base and will be deposited on guides and heads. If you are in doubt about a particular reel of tape, splice a good piece to a questionable one, record across the splice and listen to both sections. For a hot, damp climate, "Mylar"-base tape is better than cellulose-acetate tape. "Mylar" is neither brittle in dry weather nor soft and rubbery in damp weather. Thin "Mylar" tape is comparable on a cost-per-minute basis to cellulose-acetate tape.

When you buy a *record player,* look for these qualities:

–faithful reproduction
–portability, to the extent possible without sacrificing fidelity
–mechanical dependability
–constant turntable speed
–choice of three speeds (78, 45, and 33⅓ rpm.)
–pickup arm and stylus capable of playing both standard and long-playing discs. A light pressure and fine needle are required because of the microscopic size of the grooves. The arm should also be long enough to accommodate the older 16″ radio transcriptions.

Radios are so common, and there is so little difference among standard models within a price range, that there is no need to devote space to a discussion of their characteristics. One caution, however: if your group does not have its own radio receiver, do not accept someone's cast-off model without careful examination. You will need better reception for use by a group in a sizable room with doubtful acoustics than for one or two persons in a small, carpeted, and curtained room.

nonprojected visual materials

Nonprojected materials offer a "do it yourself" approach to program enrichment. Materials which you make or mount will probably not have the slickness and scope of a film produced in Hollywood, but this is often overbalanced by the following advantages:

1. When you create, or at least collect, your own materials they are almost certain to be related directly to your goals. There will be little danger of your regarding them as a substitute for preparation or as an independent form of entertainment.

14

2. They can be adapted specifically to the local situation.
3. When members of your group make or handle materials, their participation will stimulate learning.
4. A nonprojected material can usually deal briefly and directly with a single concept. Thus a single picture or a simple flannelboard presentation may be more appropriate than a film for the attention-span and comprehension of a small child. A combination of various nonprojected materials may be used to express different aspects of a more complex frame.
5. They are less expensive to use than most projected materials.

There is such a variety of nonprojected materials, with lengthy booklets available concerning almost every type, that we shall confine ourselves to listing a few practical suggestions concerning some of the common forms.

Chalkboards. Modern chalkboards are usually green, rather than black, thus contributing to the attractiveness and eye-comfort of the room. Most leaders use them, but few have thought seriously about their possibilities.

The chalkboard is more than a place to write words and other symbols for all to see simultaneously. Even this is an important function and calls for a clean, uncluttered board with symbols legible and large enough to be visible to the entire room. Beyond this, however, chalkboards may be used to visualize many concepts and relationships through such forms as outlines, diagrams, and maps.

For example, in studying Biblical history and geography one member of your group may sketch on the chalkboard his version of a map of Palestine in relation to other lands. Other members may suggest and make revisions, then perhaps use colored chalk to indicate boundaries and divisions at different periods of history. The result can be compared with printed maps.

For more elaborate drawing, usually done prior to group meetings and covered until time for use, you will want to use tools, such as rulers, compasses, and patterns to improve and speed your work. When you want to transfer a small illustration to the chalkboard you can block off the original in squares, put the same number and arrangement of squares (but larger ones) on the chalkboard, then transfer the illustration, one square at a time, to the board. If you need to use the same illustration many times you may prefer to outline it on heavy tracing paper and perforate the outline at regular intervals one inch or less apart. Then you can hold the pattern against the board and rub a dusty eraser across the perforations, thus transferring to the board an outline of chalk dots which can now be connected, freehand, with chalk.

Another method of enlarging small illustrations is to focus an opaque projector on the board and simply outline the projected image. It is also helpful to learn to draw "stick figures" of other pictures using only essential features.[3]

Flat Pictures. Flat or still pictures are among the most accessible and least expensive of all audio-visual materials. Usable illustrations can be found in most periodicals and others are available from commercial and educational distributors. They can be passed around a group and examined carefully by individuals. Children especially enjoy drawing or painting their own pictures, sometimes in such terms as "stained-glass" windows, and when they do, the value of the experience is increased both for the child, because of participation, and for the leader who can thus learn about the child from his creation.

Flat pictures can provide variety which helps to prevent stereotyping. Series of Biblical films, featuring the same casts, are likely to standardize the impression of a character, especially because the motion picture lends more finality to characterization than do the still arts. It may not matter whether or not a generation grows up in the belief that Don Ameche invented the telephone but it may matter a great deal what impression children get of the personality of Jesus, especially if it is a saccharine, spineless portrayal. A committee of the Division of Christian Education of the National Council of Churches, appointed to study the problems of visualizing Bible characters and Bible teachings, reported, "In art the differing presentations of Jesus make for a wholesome balance as no single one

16

is taken too realistically. In the motion picture medium the very realism may at times be a hindrance; especially children may be influenced adversely by a one-sided presentation of Christ. . . . The frequent use of flat pictures is recommended to counteract and balance the impressions gained by the film."[†]

When you want all your group to see the same, small picture simultaneously, opaque projection is the obvious solution.

Which pictures are worth showing to your group? To a great extent this is a matter of taste, of course, but there are certain generally accepted standards for selection:

1. A picture should present a single, clear center of interest related to your purpose. The main idea visualized should be apparent immediately, and this should be an idea which is relevant to your study theme. The picture should not be cluttered up with distracting or irrelevant details.

2. The picture should be truthful. For newspapers, picture selection may still be dominated by the "man bites dog" theme but you will generally want to present scenes which are typical, rather than unique or startling. To portray South Africa exclusively through pictures of witch doctors is to deceive, rather than to clarify.

3. High technical and artistic quality should characterize each picture. Photography, composition, and color should be attractive.

4. In most cases the picture should stimulate the imagination, either through suggestion of new experiences or re-creation of previous ones. This may be accomplished by implied action, or "human interest," or, in the case of more sophisticated groups, by various forms of symbolism.

5. A picture should be suitable to the age and background of your group. This is most important, of course, when a symbolic approach is used.

For neatness and effectiveness in presentation you may want to mount your pictures. Mounting is also a means of protection and will insure greater life of the picture. It involves attaching the picture to a heavier background and usually framing it with a border, or "mat." These margins should be generous, with

---

† Adapted from "Visualization of Bible Characters and Bible Teachings." Copyright 1954 by the National Council of Churches. Used by permission.

the bottom always the widest, and colors and materials should be selected to compliment the picture.

You may use any size of mounts, but for convenience in filing you will probably want to standardize them. It may be impossible to select a single size which can accommodate all pictures, but several will usually be satisfactory. Four commonly used dimensions are 8½″ x 11″, 11″ x 14″, 14″ x 22″, and 22″ x 28″.

Methods of mounting include the use of rubber cement, paste, gummed tapes, and "dry mounting." The latter is a fast, clean, and effective method which requires a special thin tissue, impregnated on both sides with an adhesive. The adhesive is dry, permitting ordinary handling, but when heated it softens sufficiently to adhere to whatever object is placed against it. In dry mounting the tissue is placed between the picture and the mount. Heat is then applied, usually with an iron, causing the picture to adhere to the mount. The tissue is available from most photographic supply stores. This process is more expensive than others but it is the most efficient and satisfactory method for mounting in quantity. Sources of detailed instruction for all types of mounting are included in the references.[4]

Other Flat Visual Symbols. Here we shall refer briefly to diagrams, charts, graphs, maps, posters, and cartoons, all of which are symbolic representations or explanations, rather than pictorial reproductions.

Diagrams and charts are condensed visual summaries of facts and ideas, clarifying relationships. Charts are primarily orderly arrangements of words and figures (see page 58), but diagrams feature lines and symbols (see page 42). Both usually require some background to be understood. The schematic diagram of your television receiver will not enable you to repair the set unless you have a knowledge of electronics. Generally, then, charts and diagrams are more useful in summary and review than in introduction of material. However, when your group begins with a body of common knowledge and your only purpose is to study relationships, charts and diagrams are appropriate. If, for example, questions arise concerning apparently overlapping responsibilities of various officers and committees with whom all are familiar, then a diagram will visualize the problem with its possible solutions for all to analyze.

So-called *turnover charts* often include not only charts and diagrams but pictures, graphs, and whatever else may be helpful for the presentation. These are mounted or printed on large sheets which are shown in sequence by flipping them over the top, where they are bound and supported in some fashion. Annual reports of group activities or proposed budgets may be presented in this way.

In making a chart or diagram (1) concentrate on key ideas and dispense with non-essentials, (2) use symbols large enough to be seen easily, (3) make it attractive through use of contrast, space, and perhaps color.

These same principles apply to *graphs*, which are a form of diagram but represent numerical data. They include (1) line graphs, probably the most accurate of all graphs and useful in plotting trends, growth, or frequency; (2) bar graphs, good for visualizing comparisons; (3) circle or pie graphs, useful for teaching the relationship of individual items to a whole; (4) pictorial graphs, using figures of varying sizes to represent large numbers. Thus, a man six inches tall may represent a population of a million; a man three inches tall or half a man six inches tall may represent a population of five hundred thousand. These are easily understood at a glance but are not precise.

Maps are another form of diagram visualizing geographical relationships. Many maps are available commercially, but homemade maps may focus on a particular area under study. One form of production is to utilize inexpensive or used light-colored window shades, painting the map with India ink or Tintex dyes. If a small map must be enlarged you may use the same procedures recommended in the previous discussion of the chalkboard. Outline maps may also be supplied a group for completion by individuals, thus promoting participation.

The *cartoon* is another graphic form of representing ideas, situations, and relationships; and it also depends upon unity, clarity, and attractiveness. Distinctively, however, the cartoon features exaggeration and humor. Its appeal is demonstrated daily in the newspapers where most readers will look for the cartoon but neglect the editorials usually found on the same page and dealing with the same issue.

This situation also illustrates a weakness of the cartoon. It is usually an oversimplification, if not an outright distortion, and may tend to establish and perpetuate stereotypes. Realizing this, however, you may use cartoons to stimulate interest but supplement them with qualifications and additional information on which to base more mature judgments. In this process you may help to develop more discriminating viewers of cartoons.

From the cartoon has developed the amazingly popular, admittedly powerful form of communication, the *comic strip* and comic book. To many critics the comic book is a form of "Seduction of the Innocents," encouraging escapism, violence, and illiteracy. Some educators, on the other hand, defend the comic book as an art form and use it in the teaching of language, science, history, the social studies, and even religion. It is claimed that the comics personalize instruction and thereby stimulate interest in subject matter and in reading generally.

Somewhere between these extremes may be found a sensible view of this controversial medium.

Many current commercial comics obviously cater to low ethical standards and even lower esthetic tastes. Even some of the strips which profess to have constructive purposes seem to be influenced by the prevailing patterns; some of the religious series, for example, are characterized by poor art and specialize in sensationalism. The comic magazine has associations, at present, which make it difficult for discriminating viewers to regard it as a worthy form for presentation of significant ideas. Nevertheless, cartoon strips, merely as sequences of related drawings, have definite possibilities as teaching tools, especially with children and persons whose reading abilities are limited. They may be used to create interest conducive to learning, after which the skillful leader will be certain to introduce supplementary materials.

Materials described in previous paragraphs—flat pictures, charts, diagrams, graphs, maps, and cartoons—may be used in preparing posters, bulletin boards, and tackboards—each involving specialized techniques which we cannot discuss in these pages, except to provide references at the end of the chapter.[5]

The *feltboard,* or flannelboard, or flannelgraph, takes advantage of the fact that wool and cotton felt will adhere to like surfaces. On a board covered with felt, various picture symbols are placed. When these symbols are made from felt or backed with felt or sandpaper, they will stay in place even when the board is in a vertical position. A presentation can be built up piece by piece, dismantled, and reassembled for review. Children especially enjoy placing the pieces on the board as a story is told. Words of quotations may be placed on the board in scrambled order for study and rearrangement. Alternative orders may also be considered—for example: "God is love" versus "Love is God."

The figure below shows a feltboard sequence used by a group of young people to focus their thinking on the relationship of their Christian faith to their occupational plans.

Many industrial organizations are using feltboards in sales work and personnel training, and the armed services have found them very effective in their "Character Education Program." At least one university professor believes that the feltboard is uniquely adaptable to the teaching of logic because it can so conveniently and effectively portray spatial designs which clarify relations between concepts. Both board and materials can be made at relatively little expense. Consult the references for suggestions.[6]

Factors influencing occupational choice include income, prestige, opportunities for advancement, leisure time, family provisions. What is missing?

When Christian commitment is considered, is it simply added to other factors?

Should it, instead, replace some factors, such as income, family considerations?

Or does it become central to all other factors? Can you suggest a more appropriate arrangement of symbols to portray the desired relationship?

Three-Dimensional Materials. Some materials add a third dimension to visual images. Their realism offers a supplementary appeal to the sense of touch. Common three-dimensional materials are objects, models, and mock-ups, globes, terrain or relief maps, and dioramas.

22

Objects are simply the real things, usually taken from their natural setting to be used by your group. Objects of art from other civilizations may contribute to intercultural understanding.

The terms, *"model"* and *"mockup"* are frequently confused, with no great loss. Each type, however, may serve a slightly different purpose. A model is a recognizable but not necessarily workable imitation of the real thing. A mockup is a workable but not necessarily recognizable imitation of selected features of the original. Models of various planes are useful in aircraft spotting; a mockup of the wiring of a plane helps in training maintenance electricians. Both models and mockups may increase understanding by enlarging small items or reducing the size of unwieldly ones. A large model of the larynx may help the speaker or singer to understand the process by which tones are initiated in the delicate vocal mechanism.

Globes and relief or *terrain maps* are really forms of models. They visualize geographical relationships and may be used for such varying purposes as explaining principles of soil conservation, studying highway problems, or planning a trip. Many visitors to Chautauqua Institution, New York, have gained a new understanding of the geography of the Holy Land by walking around the acre-sized scale model of Palestine there.

The *diorama,* or three-dimensional picture, is another form of model. From the Globe theater to television stage sets, dramatic students have been using dioramas for many years. Students of religious education have constructed many models of "typical Palestinian homes."

You will want to use three-dimensional materials when the addition of depth or substance will contribute to understanding; when it will help to see or touch an additional dimension. When you do use them, be certain they can be perceived in whatever way they are distinctive; this may mean seeing them at close range, or handling them, or operating them, as in the case of mockups. To be unable to do so is simply frustrating.

Field trips and drama combine sight and sound without projection.

The possibilities in *field trips* are so affected by the location of your group that there is no point in devoting much space to a general discussion. Museums, art galleries, parks, farms, industries, utilities, courtrooms, and legislative chambers are only a few possible destinations of trips. Exchange visits with other groups, particularly with those from different social, economic, or religious backgrounds, may be revealing and stimulating. Field trips make it possible to observe and occasionally participate in first-hand experiences, but they are less selective than more contrived materials and demand an unusual amount of advance planning and careful follow-up. Your group will have to decide in each case whether or not a proposed trip will be worth the time required.

Drama is such a distinctive audio-visual experience that we can do little more in these pages than refer to other sources for its study.[7] Dramatic forms vary from carefully rehearsed theatrical presentations to "ad-lib" role playing; all the variations have values for both actors and viewers. Drama provides an outlet for the imagination and creativity of performers, and promotes a degree of spectator-identification which gives a depth of reality to the viewing-listening experience. Drama removes distractions and telescopes time, causing us to observe human nature and relationships with rare clarity.

Recent developments in psychodrama may have diagnostic and therapeutic possibilities for your group, provided professional guidance is available. Sociodrama and role playing are simpler techniques which are very helpful in opening up problems.

As another form of drama, *puppets or marionettes* make a strong appeal to the imagination, especially of children. Featuring whimsy and fancy rather than realism, they can be used to tell stories at little risk of stereotyping characters. The construction, manipulation, and other specialized techniques involved in this ancient art form are decribed fully in other publications.[8]

projected visual materials

Desirable characteristics of projected materials include these elements:

–attractiveness. An image, projected by brilliant light onto a white screen in a darkened room, almost compels attention. Distractions are minimized and viewers are peculiarly receptive to personal influence in the privacy of the darkness.

–group visibility. The image is large enough for all to see simultaneously, small enough to be seen from a single vantage point. Various lenses can make this true, regardless of the size of the original object or activity.

Other characteristics are *not so desirable*:

–Most projected visual materials are more expensive than audio or nonprojected materials.

–A rather high level of skill is required for their effective use.

In addition to these general characteristics, each type of projected material has its own distinctive features. Before proceeding to the familiar slides, filmstrips, and motion pictures, let us consider an instrument which serves as a link between projected and nonprojected materials.

The *opaque projector* enlarges to screen-size nontransparent materials such as flat pictures, maps, and diagrams. It will project outlines, clippings, sheets of typing, and music, all of which would be difficult to transfer to the chalkboard. Collections of pictures may be mounted, perhaps joined by masking tape and fed successively into the machine in an organized sequence. Potentially, therefore, opaque projection is extremely valuable.

You may have been discouraged by the big, clumsy machines which must usually be operated comparatively near the screen. Since reflected light is used, all possible outside light must be kept from the screen, and the image is still likely to be less brilliant than in the case of transparencies. The materials projected, especially books, sometimes become overheated when held on the screen for more than a short period of time.

Despite these limitations, however, the opaque projector is such a versatile instrument and will allow you to make use of such a wealth of illustrative material at little or no cost that it will be worth your time and effort to experiment with it. In purchasing an instrument, select one which will accommodate material up to 10″ x 10″ in size, which uses a 1,000 watt lamp and has an efficient cooling system. You will want one which reflects the most possible light with the least possible heat on the projected material.

At least one manufacturer offers an adapter which will convert slide-filmstrip projectors into small opaque projectors. The effective area projected, of course, is only as large as a 2″ x 2″ slide, but even this allows the user to create many inexpensive materials.

Slides and Filmstrips. Like the opaque projector, slide and filmstrip projectors make use of still pictures and other flat visual materials, but only after they have been converted into transparencies. Thus, production of materials for a single user is more complicated than in opaque projection, but duplication in quantity is made possible and projection is simplified.

Most modern slides are 2″ x 2″, the size popularized by the 35 mm. camera, although the older 3¼″ x 4″ size is still used occasionally, especially when slides are made by hand.

A filmstrip resembles a series of slides; it is a related sequence of still pictures or images on a single strip of 35 mm. film. Filmstrips are also available in two sizes, single or double-frame. Most projectors accommodate both types, but almost all commercially produced filmstrips are single-frame, making each transparency about half the size of a 2″ x 2″ slide.

Slides and filmstrips can be compared thus:

Slides	*Filmstrips*
1. Less expensive to produce *singly* than motion pictures or filmstrips.	1. Less expensive to produce *in quantity* than motion pictures or slides.

2. So easily produced and such a variety available that individual slides may be woven directly into local unit of work.

3. Sequence of slides can be revised for various showings; time can be allowed during showing for discussion.

2. Can be moved quickly and simply through projector, especially desirable when accompanied by disc or tape.

3. When script is presented live, rather than recorded, time can be allowed for discussion.

Both slides and filmstrips are limited by their inability to portray motion. Photographers and artists often suggest action, but their products remain essentially *still* pictures, and not motion pictures. A slide-set or filmstrip is not a cheap movie; it is comparable to a news column, or an editorial, or a nonfiction book rather than a short story or novel; it will often approach the function of a documentary but seldom that of the drama. Slides and filmstrips are less likely than motion pictures to involve emotions and influence attitudes, but they are often at least as effective as motion pictures in conveying information and stimulating discussion.

The influence of the sound motion picture also causes some local users of slides and filmstrips to think that every accompanying script should be recorded in advance. This is not necessarily wise, especially in the case of slides. Unless you have a slide projector with automatic feed, you will need careful rehearsing to change the slides according to the rigid time pattern demanded by a recording. For this reason it is always precarious to send an accompanying record or tape to be used elsewhere by someone unfamiliar with your slides.

Even when you can overcome the mechanical problems you may not want to sacrifice flexibility for a smooth production. "Live" narration may not sound so "professional" as a record but it can be varied in speed, interrupted when desired, and adapted to the response of your group. Sometimes, of course, the script will call for interpretation, sound effects, and music which can be provided only through reheresals and advance recording. Then you may want to play the recording during a first showing of the filmstrip or slide-set, but have only informal comments, questions, and discussion accompany a reshowing of selected slides or frames.

The photography involved in making slides is a fascinating study in itself and is covered in publications listed among the references.[9] It is advisable to mount your slides between glass plates, both for their protection and to prevent their popping out of focus under projection heat. The plates may be taped together by hand or inserted in slide binders available commercially.[10]

You may also be interested in producing your own filmstrips, although slides will be at least as satisfactory for most purposes and no more expensive unless you wish to duplicate them for distribution. You may, of course, have your developed 35 mm. film returned to you in (double-frame) strip form but you are not likely to have a perfect roll in correct sequence. Filmstrips are usually made either from color transparencies or from black and white prints of uniform size. For directions as to how to produce and print your own filmstrips consult the resources at the end of the chapter.[11]

If you want to make your own slides by hand, you will probably use the older 3¼" x 4" size because you will have so much more workable area than in the newer 2" x 2" size. You will have your choice of many types, including clear, etched, or gelatin-coated glass, as well as plastic, cellophane, or silhouette cutouts.[12]

Filmstrips can also be handmade, by drawing in ink on clear film, but this is very delicate work and impractical for most situations.

Since most groups will be using both slides and filmstrips, a combination slide-filmstrip projector will be most economical. In selecting one, look for these features:

–at least a 300 watt lamp—more wattage if your showings are to be seen by more than about one hundred people or if almost all extraneous light cannot be removed.
–efficient cooling system.

–appropriate lens. Most such projectors are equipped with a 5″ projector lens, which is satisfactory for moderate-sized rooms, but if you expect to use the machine in a large auditorium also, it will be wise to purchase an additional longer lens, perhaps 7″.

–efficiency of the lens system. You can compare the light output of various projectors with an ordinary light meter.

–slide carriage: ease in changing.

–filmstrip mechanism: it should support projected frames firmly enough to prevent them from going out of focus when heated.

Some projectors are equipped with automatic feed, remote-control frame change, or filmstrip-tape synchronization. Each feature could be desirable under some circumstances, but for most groups they are all unnecessary luxuries.

A variation of the slide projector is the *overhead transparency projector*, which is operated from the front of a room, rather than the back. The leader faces the group and writes or indicates important points on a plastic transparency which is projected on a mirror, which in turn reflects the image on a screen placed behind or in front of him. Writing on the plastic surface is done with a china-marking pencil and is wiped off with cleansing tissue. Most of these machines can be supplied with an adapter making possible the use of both 2″ x 2″ and 3¼″ x 4″ slides.

Motion Pictures. Motion pictures, commonly called simply "films," can be more realistic and more attention getting than other projected materials, but they are also likely to be less flexible and more expensive.

The illusion of motion, added to sight and usually sound, provides an element of *reality* which compels attention and involves emotions. The driver who has once had a serious auto accident may push the accelerator with careless vigor years later and statistics of traffic fatalities are not likely to lessen the pressure, but the film of an accident will probably revive his memory and influence his foot, at least temporarily.

Films not only portray actions but subject them to careful analysis by speeding them up or slowing them down. A flower may be seen to grow in seconds instead of in weeks; the reaction of a driver applying his foot to the brake pedal of a car may be observed in reference to the distance traveled during the process; centuries may be telescoped into minutes. These techniques, of course, may be confusing instead of helpful; a child's sense of historical time relationships is particularly subject to twisting when these techniques are employed. It is up to the leader to be aware of impressions received and to clarify them when necessary.

The movement which adds reality and attractiveness to films also makes them *less flexible* for study purposes; it establishes a tempo, especially in dramatic productions, which cannot be interrupted without annoying observers. Unlike slides and filmstrips, films can seldom be stopped for discussion, nor can they be shown at varying speeds to suit the background of the viewers. To overcome this drawback many instructional films are being produced with accompanying filmstrips to be used at a more leisurely pace in follow-up sessions; a few are produced with unresolved endings to stimulate discussion. You may also wish to show a film a second time, substituting for the original sound track your own commentary or observations from your group.

Motion pictures are the *most expensive* type of audio-visual material because of their cost of production. A good sound filmstrip may be produced for national distribution at a cost of several thousand dollars, but $10,000 to $50,000 will be a modest budget for a film with a comparable theme. This is why the rental fees seem to be high for use by small groups. They are not actually out of line with production costs, nor necessarily high in comparison with other expenditures of groups. If you will remember your outlay for printed materials or a party the film rentals won't seem exorbitant. Consider also the "cost per impression." If a film renting for eight dollars is shown to one hundred people it has cost only eight cents for each person to see it. Compare this with entertainment admission figures or even with the cost of operating a church! The Communications Research Project of the National Council of Churches revealed that in the churches of New Haven, Connecticut, it costs seventy cents for every personal contact. In other words, the budget, divided by the number of contacts in Sunday School, church, organizational meetings, and pastoral calls, yields a cost-per-impression of about seventy cents. On that basis, film rentals are not out of line, especially since good films probably constitute the most satisfying esthetic experience in the field of group communications. On the other hand, this does not automatically justify every film rental cost for every situation. If a certain film rents for eight dollars per showing and you can purchase for five dollars a filmstrip on the same theme which can be used many times by your group, you will have to evaluate the relative merits of the materials in view of your purpose and your budget.

The mechanical problems involved in showing films have been a bugaboo in many local groups. *Careful advance preparation*, however, as described in Chapter 3, will almost eliminate them.

There are many motion picture projectors now available which operate efficiently and will give almost trouble-free service. You will want one which uses a 750 or 1,000 watt bulb, has an effective cooling system, operates as quietly as possible, and is rugged mechanically. If you plan to use many different projectionists you will also want to consider simplicity of threading and operation.

Local motion picture *production* is difficult and few will want to attempt it, but in rare cases it will serve a purpose. Resources are listed at the end of the chapter.[13] If you do attempt your own production and want to add a sound track, you may simply use a separate tape recorder, or, for better synchronization of sight and sound, you may want to consider a combination projector-recorder which utilizes a narrow stripe of magnetic material on otherwise silent 16 mm. film. This allows you to record on your film while viewing it, to make as many changes as desired, and to play it back on the same equipment.

Television. Television offers resources even beyond the range of motion pictures, featuring greater immediacy and less expense. Like radio, however, television confronts the leader with scheduling problems. In rare cases you may be able to show your group desired programs after they have been telecast by arranging with the station to borrow a kinescope, which can be shown on an ordinary 16 mm. sound projector. Magnetic tape recordings of both the sound and picture of telecasts, to be played back through a television receiver, should eventually simplify such delayed use of programs. Meanwhile, however, your group may find great value in viewing selected "live" programs and then discussing them. The "selected" programs need not always be those produced for educational or religious purposes; there are cultural implications in all the output of the mass media, and your group can profit from discriminating analysis of every type of program.

"Closed circuit" television, which is essentially an audio-visual intercommunications system, also offers possibilities for many institutions. Pictures and sound can be transmitted by cable from one room to screens and loudspeakers located in other rooms. Among its uses, closed-circuit television makes it possible to show any of the materials described in this chapter simultaneously to groups gathered in various locations connected by cable with the place where the presentation is being made.

RESOURCES, CHAPTER TWO

1 *Increasing the Effectiveness of Teaching with Tape Recording*, 10 mm. sound motion picture, b. & w., Minnesota Mining and Manufacturing Company, St. Paul 6, Minnesota. Also available from same company: pamphlet, *Tape Recording in the Classroom*.

Le Bel, C. J. *Fundamentals of Magnetic Recording*, 1951, Audio Devices, Inc., 444 Madison Avenue, New York 22, N. Y. Also available from the same corporation: the periodical, *Audio Record* and the pamphlets, *How to Make Good Tape Recordings, The Teacher Talks About Sound Recording, Standards for Educational Recording Machines,* and *Quick Facts on Magnetic Tape Recorders* (an annual directory).

---

2 The following types of equipment are produced by the manufacturers indicated, with their addresses listed below:

tape recorders—Ampex, Ampro, Bell, Bell and Howell, Berlant, DuKane, Fairchild, Magnecord, Pentron, Presto, RCA, Revere, Webster-Chicago.

record players—Bogen, Califone, Newcomb, RCA, Rek-O-Kut, V-M, Webster-Chicago.

slide and filmstrip projectors—American Optical, Argus, Bell and Howell, DuKane, Eastman, Keystone, Revere, SVE, Viewlex.

opaque and overhead projectors—American Optical, Bausch and Lomb, Beseler, Keystone, Screen Scriber, Spencer Optical, Squibb-Taylor.

16 mm. sound motion picture projectors—Ampro, Bell and Howell, De Vry, Eastman, RCA, Victor Animatograph.

35 mm. cameras—Argus, Bolsey, Eastman, Exacta, Leica, Revere.

16 mm. motion picture cameras—Bell and Howell, Bolex, Eastman.

closed circuit television equipment—
Blonder-Tongue, Dage, Farnsworth, General Precision, Kay Lab, RCA.

American Optical Co., Chelsea 50, Mass.
Ampex Electric Corporation, 934 Charter St., Redwood City, Calif.
Ampro Corporation, 2835 N. Western Ave., Chicago 18, Ill.
Argus, Inc., Ann Arbor, Mich.
Bausch and Lomb Optical Co., 626 St. Paul St., Rochester 2, N. Y.
Bell Sound Systems, Inc., 574 Marion Rd., Columbus 7, Ohio.
Bell and Howell Co., 7100 McCormick Rd., Chicago 45.
Berlant Associates, 4917 W. Jefferson Blvd., Los Angeles 16, Calif.
Beseler Co., 60 Badger St., Newark 8, N. J.
Blonder-Tongue Laboratories, Inc., 526 North Ave., Westfield, N. J.
David Bogen Co., Inc., 663 Broadway, New York 12, N. Y.
Bolex-Paillard Products, Inc., 265 Madison Ave., New York 16, N. Y.
Bolsey Corporation of America, 118 E. 25th St., New York 10, N. Y.
Califone Corporation, 1041 N. Sycamore Ave., Hollywood 38, Calif.
Dage Division of Thompson Products, 69 N. Second St., Beech Grove, Indiana.
DeVry Corporation, 1111 Armitage Ave., Chicago, Ill.
DuKane Corporation, St. Charles, Ill.
Eastman Kodak Co., Rochester 4, N. Y.
Exacta Camera Corporation, 40 W. 29th St., New York 1, N. Y.
Fairchild Recording Equipment, 154th St. and 7th Ave., Whitestone 57, N. Y.
Farnsworth Electronics Co., Fort Wayne, Indiana.
General Precision Laboratory, Pleasantville, N. Y.
Kay Lab, 5725 Keurney Villa Rd., San Diego 12, Calif.
Keystone View Co., Meadville, Pa.
Leica: E. Leitz, Inc., 468 4th Avenue, New York 16, N. Y.
Magnecord, Inc., 1101 Skilborrn Ave., Chicago 24, Ill.
Newcomb Audio Products Corporation, 6824 Lexington Ave., Hollywood 38, Calif.
Pentron Corporation, 788 Tripp St., Chicago 24, Ill.
Presto Recording Corporation, P. O. Box 500, Paramus, N. J.
Radio Corporation of America, RCA Victor Division, Camden 2, N. J.
Rek-O-Kut Co., 38-01 Queens Blvd., Long Island City 1, N. Y.

Revere Camera Co., 230 E. 21st St., Chicago 16, Ill.

Screen Scriber, Visual Training Aids, 180 W. Randolph St., Chicago, Ill.

Society for Visual Education, Inc., 1345 W. Diversey Pkway, Chicago 14.

Spencer Optical Co., 141 Fulton St., New York 38, N. Y.

Squibb-Taylor, Inc., 1213 S. Akard St., Dallas, Texas.

V-M Corporation Benton Harbor, Mich.

Victor Animatograph Corporation, Davenport, Iowa.

Viewlex, Inc., 35-01 Queens Blvd., Long Island City 1, N. Y.

Webster Chicago Corporation, 5610 Bloomingdale Ave., Chicago 39, Ill.

Manufacturers of screens, storage cabinets, and projection tables are listed at the end of Chapter 4.

For specifications of equipment, see *Audio-Visual Equipment Directory*, 1955, NAVA, 2540 Eastwood Ave., Evanston, Ill.

---

3 *Chalkboard Utilization*, 15-min. sound motion picture, b & w., University of Wisconsin, Madison, Wis.

McIntyre, Bruce, *Audio-Visual Drawing Program*, 548 S. Reece Place, Burbank, Calif., 1952.

Make Your Chalk Talk, 56-frame filmstrip, United World Films, 1942.

Making Your Chalk Teach, 47-frame filmstrip, Wayne University, Detroit, Mich., 1951.

---

4 Hoeltzel, Russell R., "Unlimited: Use of Flat Pictures," in *VEF Newsletter*, April, 1955.

Wet Mounting Pictorial Materials, 11-min. motion picture, b. & w. or color, Indiana University, Bloomington, Ind.

---

5 East, Marjorie, *Display for Learning: Making and Using Visual Materials* (New York: Dryden Press, 1952).

How to Keep Your Bulletin Board Alive, 32-frame filmstrip, color. Teaching Aids Laboratory, Ohio State University, Columbus, Ohio, 1950.

Lettering, available from Higgins Ink Co., 271 Ninth St., Brooklyn 15, N. Y.

Modern Lettering and Poster Design, as well as charts of basic lettering, available from C. Howard Hunt Pen Co., Camden, N. J.

Display letters for posters may be secured from Eagle Supply Co., 327 W. 42nd St., New York 36, or from the Redikut Letter Co., 6519 W. Boulevard, Inglewood 3, Calif.

---

6 *How to Make and Use the Feltboard*, 45-frame filmstrip, color, Teaching Aids Laboratory, Ohio State University, Columbus, Ohio.

The Feltboard and Flannelgraph, pamphlet, Ohio State University, Columbus, Ohio.

The Feltboard in Teaching, 9-min. motion picture, color, Wayne University, Detroit, Mich., 1951.

[7] Albright, H. D., Halstead, W. P. and Mitchell, L., *Principles of Theater Art* (Boston: Houghton Mifflin, 1955).

Burger, Isabel B., *Creative Play-Acting* (New York: A. S. Barnes, 1950).

Ehrensperger, Harold, *Conscience on Stage* (Nashville: Abingdon Press, 1947).

Moreno, J. L., *Psychodrama* and other publications, Beacon House, Beacon, N. Y.

Smith, Milton, *Play Production* (New York: Appleton-Century-Crofts, 1948).

Ward, Winifred, *Creative Dramatics,* 1930, and *Playmaking with Children,* 1947 (New York: Appleton-Century-Crofts).

---

[8] Batchelder, Marjorie H., *The Puppet Theatre Handbook* (New York: Harper, 1947).

How to Make a Puppet, 12-min. motion picture, b. & w., or clor, Bailey Films, 1953.

Puppetry Journal, official journal of the Puppeteers of America, published at Western College, Oxford, Ohio.

---

[9] *How to Make Good Pictures,* and *Slides,* both Eastman Kodak Co., Rochester 4, N. Y., 1949.

---

[10] Erie Scientific Corporation, Buffalo, N. Y.
Golde Manufacturing Co., Chicago 7, Ill.

---

[11] *Making Filmstrips with Amateur Equipment,* booklet, Eastman Kodak Co., Rochester 4, N. Y.

Simplified Filmstrip Production, 40-frame filmstrip, b. & w., Teaching Aids Laboratory, Ohio State University, Columbus, Ohio, 1952.

---

[12] Hamilton, G. E., *How to Make Handmade Lantern Slides,* Keystone View Co., Meadville, Pa., 1942.

How to Make Handmade Lantern Slides, 22-min. motion picture, color, Indiana University, Bloomington, Ind., 1947.

---

[13] *How to Make Better Movies,* Eastman Kodak Co., Rochester 4, New York.

Offenhauser, William H., Jr., *16 mm. Sound Motion Pictures,* Interscience Publishers, Inc., 1949.

Spottiswoode, R. J., *Film and Its Technique* (Berkeley: University of California Press, 1952).

Tips on Movie-Making, booklets, Bell and Howell Co., 7100 McCormick Rd., Chicago 45, Ill.

3

how to use them effectively

From the previous chapters it is obvious that various types of audio-visual materials have potential usefulness for many different purposes. The realization of these possibilities will depend on a number of factors, beginning with your ability to secure particular items for your situation.

locate appropriate materials

If you are going to make your own materials, or go on a field trip, or engage in role playing, you need no outside help. The possibilities will be as extensive as the imagination and resources of your group. The search itself may be an important learning experience, as when children are asked to look through magazines for pictures illustrating each of the Ten Commandments.

When you wish to consider using materials produced elsewhere, the problems of selection are more complicated, especially in the projected field where thousands of productions are available and more appear each month.

Where can you find them? Evaluation services and catalogues, such as are listed at the end of this chapter, can be of some assistance and will probably be available in your region at a public library, a state university, a YMCA, a religious publishing house or a council of churches, especially if one of these institutions operates its own audio-visual library. You will also get suggestions from friends who have used materials and from reviewers whose opinions you respect. Producers and distributors publish lists, of course, but their descriptions of materials are likely to be more promotional than analytical.

To avoid disappointment with the judgment of someone else, you will ordinarily want to preview all likely possibilities, preferably in the company of several members of your group. No one who does not know your group can give you an absolutely reliable evaluation for your situation. Previewing is time-consuming and often difficult to arrange, but there is no substitute. Most distributors will allow you to preview materials without charge at the location of a library; many of them will mail materials for preview on payment of a service fee.

If your search uncovers several possible items you can best compare their relative merits by relating them to the purposes and characteristics of your group.

What's best for your purpose? Do you want to provide an experience which emphasizes *sight, sound or both?* Does your adult group want to find out what young people really think about parental authority? Then a tape recording of such a teen-age discussion will be helpful. Does your group need geographical background for the study of an unfamiliar part of the world? Then maps with perhaps slides or a filmstrip will provide the desired visual emphasis. Are you looking for a life situation with visualization, sound, and silence in natural proportions? You will turn then to motion pictures, television, or drama.

Is the intended learning experience to be primarily *intellectual or emotional?* It is impossible, of course, to divorce these two aspects of life but at times you may concentrate on merely conveying information; at other times you may hope to influence attitudes by appealing to the whole person.

In general, the more emotional an experience is desired for your group, the greater the likelihood that a motion picture or recording will serve best; films involve the highest degree of reality and recordings employ imagination. The more intellectual the emphasis, the wiser it would seem to turn to slides, filmstrips, diagrams or nonprojected materials, all featuring flexibility and facilitating give-and-take with leader and group.

In your explorations, do not overlook "off-beat" possibilities. One leader selected a simple documentary film of a child at play for use as the central element of a worship service on the theme of becoming as children to enter the kingdom of God. Presentation of the film prepared beautifully for a meditation on childlike characteristics of enthusiasm, wholeheartedness, freedom from anxiety, confidence in others, and willingness to turn to them for help. The film had not been produced with this purpose in mind, but the leader sensed its possibilities because his goals were clearly formulated. Such careful selection contrasts sharply with the haphazard approach typified by the question most frequently asked audio-visual librarians, "What's a good movie I can show my kids Sunday?"

What's best for your group? Not only the purposes but the characteristics of your group must be kept in mind in selecting a specific material.

Will your group understand it? Knowing the intellectual level of your group, will this material be clear to them? Are its parts logically related, either through plot, inherent framework, or outline? Are the details clear? Are there too many of them? Don't choose a material which will choke your group on the mere quantity of items; there is a saturation point beyond which additional facts are largely wasted. Learn to estimate this point for your group.

Repetition sometimes aids comprehension, but this is not an argument for captions which duplicate narration. Captions on filmstrips may reinforce narration by summarizing parts of it, but complete duplication of captions and narration is offensive to most people. This is not to say that captions should ever be totally different from the narration; this would split attention and hinder development.

Be cautious in selecting films or recordings featuring fancy techniques, especially for use with children. Studies show that too many optical and sound effects confuse young viewers.

Will they believe it? Knowing your group's background of experience, will this material appear to correspond with reality? When possible, avoid straining their credulity by showing films far below their standard of dramatic quality. Be wary of sound filmstrips which attempt to tell a story, then shatter all illusion by using intermittent "bongs" to signal for a frame change; close-up "stills" of persons supposedly addressing your group from the screen are equally annoying. On the other hand, studies of motion pictures indicate that lip-synchronization (portrayal of the moving lips of speakers as dialogue is heard) is not always essential to achieving believability; it is often acceptable for a narrator to comment on scenes as they are portrayed and report the dialogue.

Will they see themselves in it? Each member of your group should react to a material by thinking, "That's the sort of thing which can happen to me." Look for items involving at least one character with whom members of your group may identify themselves; look for scenes portraying economic and social circumstances similar to those experienced by your group, unless you are deliberately introducing them to unfamiliar surroundings.

Will they respect it? The reputation of the producer, performers, and the production will affect the reception of a material. Respected roles are influential and these vary with groups: the clergy may be respected by one group and suspected by another; a Hollywood star may expect immediate acceptance by one group but will be almost unknown to another; a news commentator may be regarded as courageous and forthright by one group, as either left-wing or reactionary by another. Look for materials which feature personalities respected by your group.

Will it appeal to them? You know your group's special interests and level of sophistication. Will this material have esthetic appeal to them?

Some materials use the appeal of humor and you will have to decide whether the humor is appropriate for your purpose and your group. If you find difficulty in incorporating humor into your personal presentations to your group you may find that such audio-visuals will provide a flavorful "light touch" to your leadership. On the other hand, if you customarily employ humor in your programming leadership, you may not need to look for materials using a similar approach.

Whatever materials you use should be artistically worthy of your theme. There is no denying that there is an abundance of garish art and technical weakness in religious and educational audio-visuals. Standards are being raised, however, and will be raised more rapidly as more discriminating users of materials make their desires known to producers. Remember, too, that some criticism is primarily a form of intellectual snobbishness and should not prevent the use of an audio-visual which is something less than ideal. Productions which cannot possibly stir emotions to new depths or entertain hilariously may very well be used to convey information or stimulate discussion. Imperfect, low-budget productions should not be compared with Hollywood spectacles but with imperfect leaders and alternate techniques available to them.

Will you have time to use it properly? If your group meets for only one hour, don't plan to show a film which runs fifty minutes and requires discussion for clarification and implementation. The temptation is to omit the discussion and thereby lose much of the value of the film.

Is it worth the cost? Taking your group's budget into account, compare costs of various materials. Will a particular item be worth the expense, as well as the time and effort required to incorporate it into your program?

check physical arrangements in advance

Once you have selected a material, be certain that it will be available when you wish to use it. In the case of motion pictures to be rented, this often means reserving them several weeks or even months prior to the date of showing.

Some time before you use the material with your group you will want to see and-or hear it under the exact conditions which will prevail at the time of the meeting. If it is a non-projected item you will be certain that there is sufficient light available and that the material is plainly visible from all positions which will be occupied in the room. If it is a recording or projected material or both, your problems multiply and you will need to make many provisions.

General Provisions

1. Be thoroughly familiar with all equipment yourself or have a capable operator rehearse with you and participate with you in the actual presentation. Most pieces of equipment have clearly written manuals of operating instructions, and time spent learning smooth operation will save many man-hours of your group's study time, which would otherwise be wasted in delays and breakdowns.

2. Check the physical condition of the materials to be used, especially filmstrips or records. Don't be caught unawares by a torn filmstrip or broken-down record groove.

3. Provide for adequate ventilation in the room to be used. Even a darkened room need not become a Turkish bath.

4. Locate adequate electrical outlets, with alternating current if required. If they are not conveniently placed, secure a sufficient length of extension cord.

5. Avoid placing cords where people will trip over them. Cover them when they must be exposed on the floor. Near the projector or record-player, loop the cord around a firm support to prevent accidental dislodging of the machine.

6. If a script is to be used for narration, or for timing the showing of slides or filmstrip, provide adequate light for the reader. If there is to be a narrator in front of the room and an operator in the rear, have separate scripts or, if this is impossible, arrange for an unobtrusive system of signals between them.

Provisions for Sound

1. Place your loudspeaker, if possible, near the screen, at a height about ear-level, directed toward the center of the group. Be certain the sound is loud enough to be heard easily by most people, but not so loud as to produce listener-fatigue.

2. If a recording is to be used with a filmstrip, rehearse synchronization of the recording with the frame changes.

Provisions for Sight

1. Arrange seating so that viewers will be no nearer than two screen widths from the screen, no further away than six screen widths. Keep viewers' seats within about a thirty-degree angle of an imaginary line drawn perpendicular to the center of the screen; it should be even narrower if you are using a beaded screen. Diagonal seating in a rectangular room provides more usable viewing space but is generally inconvenient to arrange unless necessary. See diagram below.

2. Avoid having a center aisle in the room to be used. To allow

people to be seated there, place projector at the rear of the room and elevate it on a stand about four feet in height (unless you are using the unusual system of "rear projection," which operates from behind a transparent screen).

3. Remove dirt and grease from optical surfaces and other areas affecting projection, using lens-cleaning tissue and fluid, if necessary.

4. Focus the projection beam high enough on the screen to be seen easily by all viewers, provided this does not result in a projection angle greater than eighteen degrees from the horizontal (which would cause part of the picture to be out of focus).

5. If you plan to use both horizontal and vertical slides, test both carefully and locate the projector at a point which will allow either to be encompassed by the screen without repositioning the projector.

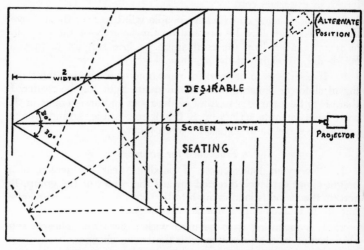

6. In motion picture projection carefully recheck the threading of the film. First operate the mechanism manually to be certain the sprockets are engaged, then, with the motor running and the sound up, be certain that the film moves firmly past the sound scanning drum to avoid a disconcerting bubbling sound. If the film involves lip-synchronization, be certain that lip movement corresponds with accompanying syllables. If not, change the size of the loop between the point of projection and the sound drum. If, during trial operation, a film loop is lost and the pictures begin jerking, look for a succession of damaged sprocket holes in the film. If possible, splice them out; if splicing would interfere with the sound track or is con-

trary to your agreement with the film distributor, at least be alert to restore the loop quickly with a minimum of interference when showing the film to your group. If possible, have a spare projector available. Be sure to have extra projection and excitor lamps and know how to replace them. Be certain the take-up reel is large enough to accommodate the film you are using.

After testing the material under actual room conditions cue it so that it will begin as desired.

At this point some leaders will believe they are ready to use an audio-visual material. A motion picture, let us say, has been carefully selected and all possible precautions have been taken to guarantee a showing which will be free from distractions. What more needs to be done? Actually, the most important preparations are yet to be made.

It must be admitted that audio-visual materials used by themselves, without careful planning by a leader, can provide learning experiences. A motion picture which is authentic and moving, even though selected at the last minute, unrelated to the group's study theme and shown without comment or discussion, may be more meaningful than a lecture by a poorly prepared leader. The same film, however, might have contributed a great deal more to the group if it had been shown at a different time when it could have been woven into the ongoing program structure and related more directly to other experiences of the viewers.

For effective use, then, you must decide exactly when during your session you will want to use the material. It may be most helpful to introduce a subject, to enrich it or to review it. It may be satisfactory for any of these functions, and its placement will depend upon the readiness of your group and other resources you plan to use.

Whenever you use it you will want to do more than just show it or play it. Communication is not a one-way process; it is a sharing. The use of audio-visual materials should not crowd out the interplay of personalities. The more personal the medium, the more effective it is in influencing attitudes. As leader of your group it is your responsibility to enhance the personal, communicative power of a material in every way possible.

You can help your group to get the most out of a viewing or listening experience by planning an introduction and a follow-up. A typical introduction will raise questions to be considered in the audio-visual presentation; a follow-up will not consist of the question, "How did you like the movie?" but may begin where the film stopped and go on from there. This approach will help to overcome one big danger: the tendency of groups to identify audio-visuals, especially projected ones, with the "escape" aspect of the mass media. A generation constantly exposed to the murder mysteries, situation dramas, variety shows, and give-away programs of commercial radio and television may be unprepared to regard a film or recording as anything but an escape from the usual pattern of group meetings. It can be much more, as you can demonstrate with intelligent introductions and follow-ups.

prepare your group

Regardless of your specific purpose you will want your group to be receptive to the viewing or listening experience. You can help to develop this attitude by establishing the authenticity of the material to be used. In most cases, too, you will want to preface the use of the material by relating its theme to the interests and needs of your group. Occasionally you will make an exception to this practice if you have selected a particular audio-visual to arouse interest or influence attitudes and if you are convinced that preceding comment would only dull its impact.

In many instances you will want to make brief explanations concerning the material: definitions of unfamiliar terms and acknowledgments of obvious shortcomings. If the audio-visual has a glaring technical weakness it is better to discount it in advance.

Beyond this point, preparation of your group will depend upon your purpose. If group members have not participated fully in the formulation of objectives, you may immediately share with them your intended purpose when your aim is concept development, deepening of understanding, or stimulation of discussion. However, when the aim involves attitude change, motivation or inspiration, specific purposes probably should not be stated to the group, lest those initially opposed to your position raise their defenses.

You will sometimes want to direct the observation of your group to specific aspects of the material, especially when your purpose is to convey concepts or deepen understanding. Studies indicate that this will result in increased learning in the areas to which attention has been directed, although other areas then seem to suffer somewhat. You may want to set up "buzz" groups in advance, direct the attention of each group to a different aspect of the presentation, and then arrange to share observations after the showing.

In general, then, effective introduction of a material consists of motivating your group to be as receptive, observant, and thoughtful as possible. You may find it helpful to use one or more audio-visuals in introducing another. For example, in preparing a group of children to get the most out of a filmstrip depicting customs of worship around the world, one teacher used maps, flat pictures, a chalkboard, objects, and records, all of which made the filmstrip more interesting and more understandable.

present the material

Even while the material is being seen or heard, you are not free from responsibility. For one thing, you must be receptive, observant, and thoughtful yourself. The leader who leaves the room or engages in other activities while a film is being shown cannot expect very much alertness from his group. True, you have already seen it, perhaps several times, but if it is as valuable as it should be, seeing it again may give you additional insight for the follow-up session. You may, of course, be involved in projection or narration. With materials which can be shown at varying speeds, you will want to avoid an overly rapid tempo which would force your group to "gulp" the material, but you will also avoid frustrating the more perceptive members with too slow a presentation. You may also want to pause during the viewing to carry on discussion; this will depend on whether or not the material lends itself to this sort of utilization. The ideal for your group will be participation without distraction. Discussion during viewing, as with a film-strip, for example, may be a form of participation; in other cases it may constitute distraction. You must judge and plan accordingly. In any case, observe the reactions of your group during the presentation; you will then be better prepared for the follow-up.

follow-up the material

In one church school when children were shown a film which occupied less than the total amount of available class time, the remainder of time was occupied by running the film in reverse! This entertained the children but probably de-stroyed any other values the film might have had. This is an extreme case, but there are many less spectacular instances of futile follow-ups, all evidencing a misconception of the place of audio-visuals in the learning process.

The crucial point in the use of an audio-visual often comes *after* the viewing or listening experience. "Follow-up" may be an inaccurate term because what follows is not a separate activity but a continuation of the learning experience which began before the material was seen or heard. No matter what you call it, be certain that the study session continues beyond the observation of an audio-visual.

This continuation may occupy more of your group's time than the audio-visual material itself. Suppose, for example, that you show a single flat picture or slide, portraying family tension in terms of a father and mother confronting a teen-age girl. The parents are determined, the girl is defiant. Initial viewing of the scene is a matter of seconds, but it can lead to a thoughtful consideration of such questions as:

What do you think is happening in this scene?
What led up to the present disagreement? How do you think it started?
What sort of parents are these? What kind of home is it?

46

Is there any value in anger?
When are children old enough to make their own decisions?
What should the girl do now? the parents?
Who can help this family? How?
How will this scene affect future family life?
How can such antagonisms be avoided?

A discussion along such lines will develop insights into the feelings and motivations of others and of viewers themselves. A follow-up, then, will be related to the audio-visual material but will not be limited to it. Its nature will be dependent on your leadership aims.

If your specific purpose in using an audio-visual material is *to arouse interest,* then the presentation will serve primarily as a take-off point and the essential study will proceed in one of the directions indicated below.

If you are using the material *to stimulate discussion* you will want to do these things:

–focus attention on the central issues raised.
–call attention to undesirable customs and practices visualized. Portrayal of ineffectual personal counseling, for example, may be an excellent stimulus for a discussion of improved techniques. "What's wrong with this picture?" is an appropriate follow-up question.
–discuss the application of general principles to the local situation.
–provide supplementary materials and suggest other opportunities for further study.
–bring the discussion, when possible, to some conclusion, if only as a clarification of areas of disagreement.

You may also want to break up your larger group into smaller ones for partial and preliminary discussion.

Discussion will usually be involved also in the pursuit of each of the next two basic aims.

When your aim is informational, *to develop concepts* or deepen understanding, you will want to make these efforts:

–review the points to which attention has been directed in advance.
–supply missing or additional facts.
–relate parts of the presentation to each other, possibly through an outline on the chalkboard.
–make the group aware of the learning which is occurring, perhaps

through some form of test.

–clarify words which appear to have been misunderstood.

–relate the theme, even more directly than in the introductory session, to the interests and needs of the group.

–relate the theme to other study sessions of your group.

–be certain that errors and bias have been recognized. One filmstrip on the theme of prejudice, attempting to illustrate the fallacy in judging without knowing facts, pictured an elderly lady rocking on her front porch accompanied by the caption, "If you wanted to know about baseball, you wouldn't ask this sweet old lady." Some years after the filmstrip's release an elderly lady became famous on a network quiz program as a baseball authority. That particular frame can now be used to demonstrate that even the producers of the filmstrip could unthinkingly stereotype and categorize people!

In concept development a second showing of the material, especially if it is a motion picture, is often desirable. As suggested in earlier pages, you may want to run it without the sound track and allow your group *to exercise powers of recall and recognition.* When your purposes are other than informational the wisdom of a second showing is more open to question and will have to be determined by the feeling of the group.

When your purpose is to *influence attitudes,* the predisposition of your group will be the critical factor in determining the extent and direction of your follow-up. If you are hoping to reinforce attitudes already held, then you will encourage individuals to restate their opinions. If you are attempting to bring about a change in attitude, then you will be careful to avoid forcing any response.

When your aim is *to motivate,* you will probably favor only limited discussion but acquaint the group with specific opportunities for action.

When your purpose is *to inspire,* immediate discussion may be out of place. Instead you will provide opportunities to express feelings in worship, in song, and in action.

In many cases your aim will not be confined to a single category listed above, but will involve elements of several of them. You may also want to use the same material for varying purposes at different times. One director of religious education used the same film in his church twelve times in one year; it was used for different purposes and sometimes with different groups.

Most modern materials are accompanied by detailed leaders' guides and these will be helpful, but you will want to exercise initiative and adapt all suggestions to your own group to avoid stilted and stereotyped presentations. Occasionally it will be wise for you to record sessions in which you use audio-visual materials so that you can analyze your procedures and the reactions of the group. It is well to engage continually in re-evaluation of the materials you use and their effectiveness in the learning process.

To use audio-visuals effectively we have seen that it is necessary to prepare the materials, to prepare equipment, to prepare the group, and to prepare for the follow-up—all of which really means that the leader must be well prepared.

RESOURCES, CHAPTER THREE

Catalogs and Evaluation Services

Audio-Visual Resource Guide and Evaluation Bulletin, Visual Education Fellowship, National Council of Churches, 257 Fourth Avenue, New York 10, N. Y.

Blue Book of Audio-Visual Materials, Educational Screen, 64 E. Lake Street, Chicago 1, Ill.

Catalog of Charles G. Reigner Library of Recorded Sermons and Addresses, Union Theological Seminary, Richmond, Va.

Catalog of Radio Recordings, a Transcription Service for Schools, U. S. Office of Education, Washington 25, D. C.

Cumulative Index of Films (a separate one of filmstrips) *of Jewish Interest,* Audio-Visual Service of Yeshiva University, Amsterdam Avenue at 186th Street, New York 33, N. Y.

Educational Film Guide (a separate one for filmstrips), H. W. Wilson Co., 950 University Avenue, New York 52, N. Y.

Educational Film Library Association (evaluations available to members only), 345 E. 46th Street, New York 17, N. Y.

Ehrmann, Eliezer L., *Catalogue of Visual Aids,* 1950, Department of Supervision, Board of Jewish Education, Chicago, Ill.

Educators' Guide to Free Films (a separate one for filmstrips), Educator's Progress Service, Randolph, Wis.

Freedom Film Library, Anti-Defamation League of B'Nai B'Rith, 20 West 40th Street, New York 18, N. Y.

Guide to Film Services of National Associations, Film Council of America, 600 Davis Street, Evanston, Ill.

Guide to Films for Church and Community Use, Religious Film Libraries, connected with denominational publishing houses in various locations in the United States.

Human Relations Aids, Mental Health Materials Center, 1790 Broadway, New York 19, N. Y.

Jewish Audio-Visual Review, National Council on Jewish Audio-Visual Materials, 1261 Broadway, New York, N. Y.

National Tape Recording Catalog. Department of Audio-Visual Instruction, 1201 16th Street, N. W., Washington 6, D. C.

Sight-Sound, and *Evaluation Service*, World Council of Christian Education and Sunday School Association and RAVEMCCO, 156 Fifth Avenue, New York 10, N. Y.

Williams, Catherine M., *Sources of Teaching Materials* (including pictures, charts, maps, feltboard materials, as well as recordings and projected materials), Bureau of Educational Research, Ohio State University, Columbus 10, Ohio.

4

how to plan for others to use them

As you make use of audio-visual materials you are likely to become more and more convinced of their value. Then you will wonder why others in your organization are overlooking them. No matter what explanations are given for avoiding them, the real reason will probably be that audio-visual materials seem to be too much of a bother to use. Without denying that their use generally makes teaching more difficult, you can help to reduce this difficulty by promoting co-operative planning. When all the leaders within an organization co-ordinate their efforts in this field, the use of audio-visual materials can be made less complicated, less expensive, and more effective in terms of total impact.

The regular use of audio-visual materials by various groups within an organization involves five general areas of responsibility:

1. Selection and procurement of the audio-visual materials themselves
2. Filing and distribution of materials
3. Purchase of adequate equipment and construction of facilities
4. Maintenance and operation of equipment where and when needed
5. Acquainting leaders with availabilities and methods of use

Each organization may develop a different plan for delegating these responsibilities. Where personnel is extremely limited, a single audio-visual co-ordinator may undertake all five tasks. If this appears to be necessary, the co-ordinator should possess qualifications other than the physical strength to be able to carry motion picture projectors to various parts of a building! In an organization of any size, volunteers can be secured to assist the co-ordinator in one or more phases of his work.

In most instances it will be desirable to have a committee responsible for audio-visual education, preferably a subcommittee of the educational committee or the general program committee. This will allow the co-ordinator to receive guidance from responsible leaders and will also keep those leaders in touch with the work in audio-visual education. The committee's responsibilities may appropriately embrace all instructional materials, including printed matter.

The co-ordinator may be chairman of this committee and he will probably retain responsibility in the fifth area listed above, acquainting leaders with availabilities and methods of use. He will also be expected to submit recommendations to the committee for the purchase of materials and equipment, areas one and three.

One of the co-ordinator's assistants will be the audio-visual librarian, responsible for area two. He will catalogue and file materials, and arrange for their distribution when needed. He will also assist the co-ordinator in area one, the recommendation of materials for procurement.

A second assistant should have some technical background to enable him to accept responsibility for area four. He will be able to operate all equipment and will train others to do likewise. He will be able to repair the equipment, or at least know when and where to have it repaired. In addition, he will assist the co-ordinator in area three, recommending purchase of equipment and construction of facilities.

It is obvious that responsibilities can be re-divided or subdivided, depending on the number and interests of persons available. The following specific tasks, however, call for more careful examination.

selection and procurement of the audio-visual materials themselves

The initial step in this process will probably be the taking of an inventory. Someone, preferably the person who has agreed to be the audio-visual librarian, must locate materials already owned by your institution or organization. Materials are sometimes secured by one leader, then hidden away and seldom used by others. Valuable items are often excavated from dusty closets.

Next, it will be necessary to survey the over-all needs of your organization. You will avoid confining your selections to any single program area. Some groups, for example, own an extensive collection of square-dance records but very little else! You will also take precautions against over-balancing your library in the direction of any single type of material. Just because several leaders discover that filmstrips can be very helpful in stimulating discussion, there is no reason for you to neglect tape recordings, motion pictures, and nonprojected materials.

Should you buy or rent materials? This question will not arise in connection with nonprojected materials, which you will generally be able to make or buy at a low cost, nor will it be asked often in connection with filmstrips or records, which are seldom available on a rental basis, but it may present a real dilemma with respect to films. The cost of prints of some films, of course, is beyond the budget of most local groups, but educational producers realize that repeated use of films is often desirable and so they are attempting to make some prints available at a much lower cost than was formerly thought possible. When this is the case you will have to decide whether to rent or purchase the print on the basis of the number of uses you expect to make of the film. If you anticipate only a single use, or even several uses, it will usually be more economical to rent the film. If you envision using the film with many different groups at different times, then it may be desirable to purchase a print. Owning a print will make it possible for you to schedule its showing at the most appropriate time in the program schedule of various groups, whereas renting a film often constitutes a temptation to "get the most out of the rental fee" by inviting to the single showing many different groups, regardless of their current program interest.

The co-ordinator and librarian will secure the most satisfactory materials by consulting the leaders who will be using them. In many cases, of course, the leaders themselves will make the initial recommendations. The reactions of the entire groups using the materials are even more helpful in deciding which items to make a permanent part of the library. Previews will be scheduled for leaders, and the co-ordinator and librarian themselves will often engage in pre-previews to sift materials and select the best for consideration by the larger committee of leaders.

The cost of purchasing materials, especially projected ones, sometimes causes an organization to enter into a co-operative arrangement with other similar organizations. If the cost of films and filmstrips can be shared among a dozen clubs or churches it would seem that all could have access to more materials at less expense. In exceptional cases such an arrangement proves to be workable. Generally, however, dissatisfactions arise when several groups want to use the same item on the same date, usually a holiday or festival. Other difficulties are caused by the complexities of cataloguing and distribution. When a co-operative association, such as a council of churches, has a staff person able to undertake the responsibilities of a librarian, then the scheme can be workable. Otherwise, however, the frustrations usually outnumber the gains.

filing and distribution of the materials

When an audio-visual library or teaching-materials-center is to be used by only one organization or institution, its operation can be relatively simple. There must, however, be some filing system which will permit leaders to locate desired materials and have ready access to them. There should also be some provision for keeping a record of each use, to allow for the tracing of materials currently out of the library and to allow the co-ordinator to study the extent to which the various items in the library are used.

Some librarians prefer to use the Dewey Decimal System of cataloguing audio-visual materials as well as books, and this is probably appropriate where a single library houses both books and audio-visuals, but it is scarcely necessary for more limited collections.

A typical, simplified system will number and file each material in the order of its acquisition: FS (filmstrip) 1, FS 2, FS 3, and so on. Then an alphabetical card file will be developed, including for each material a title card and one or more other cards headed by subjects considered in the material. Your organization probably has its own program vocabulary, and you will use terms especially meaningful to your particular leaders. One group may have many cards filed under "stewardship" while that heading may be unused by another group, whose files may include such headings as "acculturation" or "permissiveness" which may not appear as a category in the first group. Each subject-card, of course, will refer to the title and file number of a particular item.

Storage is a major problem in an audio-visual library. Dust is harmful to both records and film, as well as to nonprojected materials. For preservation over a period of many years films and tape should be stored in rooms where temperature and humidity can be controlled. Efficient use of space is not a simple matter because of the varying sizes and shapes of materials, but special cabinets, built to accommodate films, filmstrips, and records, are available from suppliers listed at the back of this book.[1] Materials will be kept in marked containers, but in the case of tapes it is also wise to identify the reels with china-marking or grease pencils, and to insert the title in the white space of the leader tape. Otherwise, cartons may be exchanged and the appearance of a tape, unlike a film or filmstrip, gives no clue to its title. If pictures and tearsheets can be put on 8½" x 11" mountings they can be kept in standard files and used conveniently in modern opaque projectors.

All film should be examined periodically and spliced and cleaned when necessary.

Every audio-visual library should include not only the materials owned by a particular group but all possible catalogues, listings, and evaluations of materials available elsewhere. The librarian can then help leaders to secure materials from outside sources.

purchase of adequate equipment and facilities

This function was listed deliberately *after* rather than before the selection of materials. Many groups come to audio-visual specialists with the question, "What equipment should we buy first?" The question is premature unless someone representing the group has already studied available materials in the light of the group's program. The tendency is to think in terms of buying first a sound motion picture projector, but seldom has a group considered carefully how many films are appropriate for its needs and how often the machine will be used. In many cases the group would be wiser to begin by using nonprojected resources, then perhaps purchase a tape recorder or slide-filmstrip projector with screen, or both. When leaders are ready to schedule a number of specific films for specific purposes, then it is time to order a motion picture projector. And don't forget to consider the purchase of an opaque projector!

Chapter 2 with its resource list provided information concerning specific pieces of equipment, but there are a few general, recurring problems which deserve consideration at this point. One common question is whether an institution should set aside a single room as the "audio-visual room" and equip it rather elaborately, or plan to use materials on a more modest scale in all rooms. The second alternative is much preferable.

Using an "audio-visual room" is bad psychologically, especially with children. They go to the room as they go to the theater, and in this generation theater going is regarded primarily as an escape, not as a revealing experience. Going to the audio-visual room is usually regarded as an interruption in the course of study, rather than as one phase of it. This is not to deny that a skillful leader can make the best of the situation, and even take advantage of the spontaneous interest connected with the audio-visual room, but the same interest can usually be focused more sharply in the regular classroom.

Equipping only one room for audio-visual purposes also means that no more than one group may be using projected materials during the same session, creating a troublesome scheduling problem. Possession of only one projector may create a similar conflict. It is frequently possible to stagger projection times in order to allow the same machine to be used in different rooms at different times during a single session, but the mechanics are distracting and the leader's utilization plans must conform to the traffic plan. It is better, then, to schedule different types of materials in different classes during a single session, unless more than one projector is available. Some organizations will be able to purchase several tape recorders and filmstrip projectors to ease this situation. The cost saved by *not* devoting one room exclusively to audio-visual purposes should make possible the purchase of many pieces of equipment.

Whenever possible, then, it will be desirable to plan to use audio-visuals in the room where your group meets regularly. You should have adequate chalkboard space. For projection purposes you will want to investigate methods of darkening windows without eliminating ventilation. The roll-up shade is inexpensive but cuts out air along with light; pull-drapes are more expensive than shades but can be set out from the wall and up from the floor to allow ventilation even when drawn. They are also decorative and helpful acoustically. Full-closure Venetian blinds are more expensive than either shades or drapes but offer gradation of light control.

Screens can be mounted overhead on rollers, from where they can be pulled down to a point where the bottom reaches four or five feet from the floor. If you cannot afford to purchase screens for each room you may be able to use flat, white walls, although these are uncommon today. A more customary alternative is to use portable screens. Some of these are mounted on rollers to be attached to walls, others use tripods, and still others roll up from a bottom support. The latter type may be useful in a worship setting where you do not want the screen to be visible until time for use. It is even better, of course, to have a concealed overhead roller, or, still better, to have the unrolled screen concealed behind curtains which can be opened quickly. Dossal cloths customarily seen in the chancels of many churches can be hung to serve this purpose if you do not encounter liturgical objections.

Selection of screens for the various rooms will depend upon the dimensions of the rooms. A room approximately square should have a flat white screen, while an oblong room can use a beaded one. The latter is covered with minute glass beads and has more brilliance in the center of the room but fades more sharply than the flat white screen toward the sides. A square screen is desirable to allow for maximum use of both vertical and horizontal slides. Its width should be about one-sixth of the distance between the spot where it will be placed and the furthest point in the room from where it will be viewed. The use of too small a screen reduces attractiveness of a presentation and a larger screen tends to increase the viewers' attention span.

The size of a projected picture is affected both by the distance of the projector from the screen and by the focal length of the lens used. A 2″ lens is standard with most 16 mm. motion picture projectors and a 5″ lens is standard with most slide-filmstrip projectors. Assuming the use of those lenses for the projection of motion pictures and filmstrips, the following chart suggests screen widths for rooms of various sizes.

approximate distance: projector to screen	approximate desirable seating	screen width
22′	25	50″
31′	50	70″
43′	100	8′
53′	200	10′

To show 2″ x 2″ slides in a room listed above, you will have to position the projector much nearer the screen, unless you use either a larger screen or a 7″ lens. More detailed charts are available from projector and screen manufacturers.[2]

Your equipment should also include good projection stands.[3] They should provide *steady* support for your projectors at a height above the head level of your seated group. They should be easily portable and should contain shelf space for reel cans and scripts. A self-contained script-reading light is another desirable feature.

Your rooms should also be equipped, at the front, with permanently installed speakers which can be connected with all your sound equipment. These, or at least supports for portable speakers, should be located near the screen, at about ear level. It is very convenient to have light switches in the back of the room, near the location of the projectionist.

Darkening facilities, changes in wiring, and acoustical treatment may be difficult and costly to provide in an old building. This makes it all the more important for leaders to be alert to audio-visual needs when new buildings are contemplated.[4] By arranging for an audio-visual specialist to consult with your architect at the proper time you may be able to make great improvements in audio-visual methods at financial savings. The essential needs are simple enough: audibility, visibility, and flexibility. Insuring these, however, requires careful study of architectural plans. This is the ideal time to consider installation of closed-circuit television conduits and facilities.

maintenance and operation of equipment
where and when needed

When a co-ordinator or his assistant can assure leaders that materials will be shown for them at whatever time they designate, most reticence to use projected materials is overcome. Volunteer projectionists are relatively numerous but they must be well trained to be helpful. A technical assistant can carry on this training, as well as keep the equipment in the best of condition. All equipment should be kept in a central storage place where it may be inspected and serviced regularly. Each machine should be cleaned and lubricated (if needed) on schedule; and spare bulbs, fuses, and cartridges should be kept in stock. Efficient, dependable operators can free the leader to concentrate on the essential task of utilization.

acquainting leaders with availabilities and methods of use

An audio-visual co-ordinator must study the program plans of all groups within his organization. Then he will be in a position to recommend to leaders the use of materials which may not have come to their attention. He will, of course, keep in touch with current productions through periodicals and evaluation services.

At staff meetings the co-ordinator will keep other leaders aware of audio-visual possibilities by having new materials and brochures available for examination and by arranging for audio-visual presentations to the staff whenever appropriate. Occasionally he may encourage his colleagues to attend audio-visual workshops or, better yet, he will see to it that sessions dealing with audio-visual methods are included in conferences dealing with broader aspects of leadership training.

Such a five-fold approach to audio-visual education will cost money. Funds should be allocated and there should be a budget, set in advance by the responsible committee. It is a mistake to finance the use of audio-visual presentations with admissions or offerings or special grants for single showings. Audio-visual communication is simply one phase of the learning process of your group and should be treated accordingly; it should receive no more and no less than its share of your over-all budget. If you now have access to less money than you believe should be devoted to this purpose, your best chance to demonstrate the need for more is to concentrate on the *skillful use of appropriate materials* in the ongoing program of your group.

RESOURCES, CHAPTER FOUR

1 Neumade Products Corporation, 250 W. 57th St., New York 19, N. Y.

Wallach and Associates, Inc., 1532 Hillcrest Rd., Cleveland 18, Ohio.

2 Da-Lite Screen Co., 2705 N. Pulaski Rd., Chicago 39, Ill.

Radiant Manufacturing Co., 1202 S. Talman, Chicago 8, Ill.

3 Advance Furnace Co., 2310 E. Douglas, Wichita, Kan.

Neumade Products Corporation, 250 W. 57th St., New York 19, N. Y.

Smith System Heating Co., 212 Ontario St. S. E., Minneapolis 14, Minn.

4 *Architects' Visual Education Handbook,* Bell and Howell Co., 7100 McCormick Rd., Chicago 45, Ill.

Planning Schools for Use of Audio-Visual Materials, Department of Audio-Visual Instruction, National Education Association, 1201 16th St., N. W., Washington 6, D. C.

Ritenour, S. Turner, "Rooms and Equipment Aid Christian Education" in *VEF Newsletter,* April, 1956.